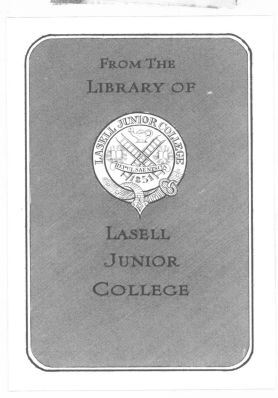

What Makes a Shadow?

WHAT MAKES A SHADOW?

By
Clyde Robert Bulla

Illustrated by
Adrienne Adams

Thomas Y. Crowell Company, New York

P.H.

LET'S-READ-AND-FIND-OUT BOOKS

Special Adviser: *DR. ROMA GANS*, Professor Emeritus of Childhood Education, Teachers College, Columbia University.

Editor: *DR. FRANKLYN M. BRANLEY*, Coordinator of Educational Services, American Museum—Hayden Planetarium, consultant on science in elementary education.

1   2   3   4   5   6   7   8   9   10

What Makes a Shadow?

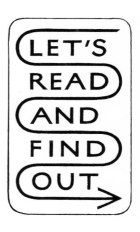

LET'S
READ
AND
FIND
OUT

The sun is shining. It shines on the trees and the side-
walk. It shines on your house.
It shines on you, too.

When the sun is in front of you, look behind you.
You can see your shadow.
When you move, your shadow moves.
When you run, your shadow runs.
But you can never catch it.

What makes the shadow? Where does it come from?

The sun is very bright. It shines on the house. It
shines on the trees. It shines on you. But the sun
does not shine THROUGH you.
There is a dark place behind you where the sun does
not shine. The darkness is your shadow.

Look for more shadows.

A tree has a shadow. The shade of the tree is the shadow of the tree.

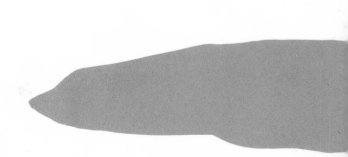

A house has a shadow.

The sun shines on one side of the house.
There is a shadow on the other side.

Animals have shadows.

So do cars.

Airplanes have shadows. Watch an airplane as it flies over your head. You may see its shadow on the ground.

A cloud has a shadow.

Sometimes the sky is dark with clouds.
The sun cannot shine through them.
The shadows of the clouds fall on the earth.
The shadows make the day dark.
We say, "This is a cloudy day."

Some shadows are darker than others.

Hold a handkerchief so the sun shines on it. The handkerchief makes a shadow on the ground. The shadow is not dark because some of the sunlight shines through.

Hold a book so the sun shines on it. The book makes
a shadow on the ground. It makes a dark shadow
because no sunlight shines through.

Watch the sun go down.

Watch the night come.

Night is a shadow.

The sun shines on one side of the earth. The other
side is in shadow. The shadow makes the night.

Inside the house at night you can see more shadows.
Hold your hand between a lamp and the wall. You
will see the shadow of your hand on the wall.

Do you know how to make a big shadow?
Hold your hand close to the lamp. The shadow is big
because your hand shuts out so much of the light.
This makes more darkness on the wall.

Move your hand away from the light. Move it farther and farther away. Now the shadow on the wall gets smaller and smaller and smaller. It is smaller because your hand does not shut out so much light. There is less darkness on the wall.

You can have fun with shadows. Hold your hands between the light and the wall and make shadow pictures. Hold them like this.

You can make a duck.

Or a rabbit.

You can hold a pencil in your hand and make an Indian with a feather.
You can make shadow pictures little or big.

You can move your hands to make the pictures move.

There are other shadow pictures
you can make.

Here are some.

Look for shadows.

How many can you find?

Can you discover what makes each shadow?

ABOUT THE AUTHOR

Clyde Robert Bulla grew up on a farm near King City, Missouri. He received his early education in a one-room schoolhouse where he began writing stories and songs. He finished his first book shortly after his graduation from high school and then went to work on a newspaper as a columnist and a typesetter.

He continued to write, and his books for children became so successful that he was able to satisfy his desire to travel through the United States, Mexico, and Hawaii. His home is in Los Angeles, and it is there that he composes his songs and writes his stories.

ABOUT THE ILLUSTRATOR

Adrienne Adams was born in Fort Smith, Arkansas, and attended Stephens College in Columbia, Missouri, and the University of Missouri. Soon afterward she became a display art director and a free-lance designer.

Miss Adams' first illustrating was done for a book written by her husband, John Lonzo Anderson. Now she is always hard at work illustrating children's books, whether on her twenty-one acre home in New Jersey or in the Virgin Islands in the winter.